port of call

Davida Singer

Plain View Press
http://plainviewpress.net

3800 N. Lamar, Suite 730-260
Austin, TX 78756

Copyright © 2012 Davida Singer. All rights reserved under International and Pan-American Copyright Conventions. No part of this book may be reproduced or distributed in any form or by any means, or stored in a data base or retrieval system, without written permission from the author. All rights, including electronic, are reserved by the author and publisher.

ISBN: 978-1-935514-98-5
Library of Congress Control Number: 2011945374

Cover art: *The Sanctity of Blue* by Lenny Foster
Cover design by Pam Knight

Acknowledgements

Special thanks to Bonita Leeds, Ellen Gray, Karen Pearlman for tender edits; to Claudia Bader for abiding wisdom; and to Michael Knight of The Helene Wurlitzer Foundation of New Mexico for precious time.

*In memory of my mother Libby, my father Benjamin
and publisher Susan Bright, who grokked it all.*

*For Isabelle who stokes the fire,
and for Iris who keeps the faith.*

Contents

millennium   9

    how to get away   11
    nocturnal   15
    as time floods like foam   17
    city poem   18
    country poem   19
    she is standing   21
    eclipse   23
    she travels in deep space   24

florida   27

    what day is this   29
    she's on vacation   30
    insomnia crawls   31
    time swings   32
    the next day   33
    love snags   34
    her dreams invert   35

montreal   37

    april 2000   39
    auberge du vieux port   40
    she lifts her pen   42
    she writes again   43
    love plays at her   44
    montreal midnight   45
    later on   47
    predawn   48

dementia   **51**

    day by day   53
    cholom   54
    cholom 2   55
    assisted living   56
    one day   58
    another day   59
    birthday   60
    something holds   61
    cusp 2003   62
    names   64
    freeze frame   65
    memorial   66

long island: east end   **67**

    country   69
    night scene   71
    m.d.   72
    diva   73
    another night   74

vermont   **75**

    blizzard   77
    snowed in   78
    what she sees   79
    what she can do   80
    what they do   81
    what she prefers   82
    what she crosses   83
    what she finds   84
    what she leaves   85
    and what she takes   86

new york   **87**

    prelude   89
    september 11 2001   90
    september 12   91
    october 1   92
    november/april 2002   93
    vertigo   94
    earlier   95
    later   96
    dementia 2001   97
    coda new york   98
    navaho 2002   99
    anima   101

taos   **103**

millennium

*Who, constructing the house of himself or herself, not for a day
    but for all time, sees races, eras, dates generations,
The past, the future, dwelling there, like space, inseparable
    together.*
                    Walt Whitman, "Kosmos," *Leaves of Grass*

how to get away

it opens here
like this
a fissure in the frame
somewhere
the middle of her life
suspended
a crackle of bone
she's restless   jumpy
wedged between
a passion past/
passion present
seeing double
a spinning blue
like in a dream
she rides her bike
down upper broadway
100th street
a stop   a pivot
the turkish restaurant
where three years
or three months later
she'll be hit
by a pedestrian
running for a bus
against the light
and fracture her pelvis
in two places   changing
how she looks at things
two women she loves
will meet   first time
in the emergency room
st. luke's hospital
where she is taken
a sequence of moments
all will follow
from there

pedaling   double time
(like in a dream)
she sees the future's fate
whiz through
a puddle by the curb
how personal reflects externals
how the fracture
of the earth's pelvis
in too many places
changes everything
she's somewhere
in the middle of her life
and she wakes
at the tuck of the century
the last bend and crease
and she's afraid
there aren't words
to describe what she saw
before the gargantuan turn
or anything left to say
there aren't words past fear
past shift
only the grip of her hands
on the bars
only the trust
only the turn

how to get away
she can't breathe
can't write here
the city   manhattan
rapid toppling length of it
the grimy brown
a flash of cobalt
between buildings
how to elevate   escape

she dreams of dancing
in a new world
dressed in black
ravened
shiny browed and lawless
renaming flight
she hunts for words/jargon
an extraordinary window
a slit along the wall
her limbs like feathers
lift and tremble
in the still
specters come alive
in her sleep

   2

south fork   long island
she's cat sitting
a fisherman's cottage/
shingled hideout
five houses from the bay
red crossbeams
stone fireplace
oak table
bedroom skylight
an easy refuge
under wraps

is it day or night
she writes
where stars drip fearless
to the ledge
where sweet sweet death
of autumn
or the first extended bough
of winter
overhangs the door

where raven spreads her wing
the outline of her body
outspoken
predicting voluminous snow
or plagues
as yet unnamed

the rafters of the cottage
where she sits
so low she wants out
almost as soon as she's in
lately   she's after reach
perspective
ready to gulp in islands
over her head
stoned on solitude
but spiky premonitions
pull her home   before sunset
penning shorthand
swift and diligent
as if the clock's pushed
as if too soon
the sprawl of dark
will fill immeasurable

nocturnal

in sleep
ravens with metallic sheen
flutter near her eyelids
she's read
they have more calls/
adaptability
than any animal
legendary
controllers of weather
prophets of calamity
but eskimos believed
ravens created light
flinging mica chips
into the sky

in dreams she flies

relentless as ravens
sleuth like
the scent of night
the sword edge glint of moon
in her hair
five houses from the beach
the earth cants cold
she hovers for a close-up
barely upright   tipsy
chasing after shadows

so now   she asks
what healing sonant
what measured notes
rite of augury
set of numbers
deck of cards
what book of runes
what kabbalistic sign
what incense burned

what candle lit
what planetary purl

she flies in dreams
trailing forecasts
ciphering time

what stroke   what speed
what mantra/meditation
air or ocean filled
what overflow
what holy fissure/destination
mode of transportation
then   what port
what port of call
can reshape/harbor destiny
before all sleek horizons
sink and fail

as time floods like foam

off the new year
she listens
tracks its cadence
from her bed
or on the island
she follows fog
full bodied apparition
tenuous and slippery
to maneuver through
but never touch

time floods
into nightmares
cities recognized
bust at the seam
refugees spill
over borders
earth withered
lakes brimmed rust
rivulets of smoke
claim continents
she sobs into armfuls of dust

millennium has come and gone
breath releases
flows on
but time and fog
skew everything gauzy
intangible
and frames of film
like signals
come unraveled
in her sleep

city poem

she wants vision
sight like raven
like never before
wants this coupling
in her mother tongue
in manhattan
where tongue and texture
graze the pavement/collide
she wants the beat
gritty cadence echoed
in her own mouth
in a city of percussion
stoops and hallways
she wants funk/disclosure
dares to swim love
like the hudson
wants this once   the edge
language stripped bare
between her fingers
like a bow stroke
fondling notes
a voice   a body solved
like mystery
she wants to ride the rim
no ceiling
like chagall
up here   upraised
above the balconies
the roofs on greenwich avenue
where they
like fliers shedding skin
leaking flame
all risk all night
expanded
wide as constellations

country poem

leaves splash languid gold
this year
in north haven
where the pond sign says
skate at your own risk
and suddenly
she wants to glide
real bad   then later
it's burgundy rush
on maidstone park road
she's feeling the vibe
like the century
and fresh romance
just went slo mo
with the woman of france
at the cottage door
indefinite accent
collar up
valiant in the eyes
that lip so curled/
so elvis   inviting sex

the gas heat kicks in
there's a cord of firewood
just in case
she holds her tender
by the waist
and it doesn't matter
any more
if the future's crouched
on the stairs
and the night's gone obsidian

2

monday night   east hampton

she watches her
she watches time/distance
her   boarding the bus
hand tented high
against the window
she watches as the bus begins
to fade   like color into rain
the hand might stretch
some more   might even wave
but there's too much dim
to be sure
the bus turns right
on main street   heading west
and steals away
she watches after autumn oaks
into nothing
for a little while
then a little longer
(car keys clink together
in her hand)
until the wanting
of that moment past
expands   begins to seize
like snarling thunder
like some just remembered pain

she is standing

in another time zone
another flame
the heat of it
never cooled
the jostle of memory/
messy spill
into the new millennium
time capsizes
she's in the thick of it
this love/this waltz
with zita
the belly up/finale
there is no bus here
no waiting
only the sound of separation
grey walls
and the shatter of flowers
in glass
they cannot touch this
there are no words
for splintered distance
in this shallow chelsea loft
they cannot make it happen
clean enough
tear fast enough
so her heart will yield
lyrical this time   because
it finally knows how
or because it knows
it can never learn
to do this right

   2

time reverses/
zooms in   shelter island
march or april
maybe 1992

when she and zita give way
a slow ebbing
of floorboards too soft
to keep them afloat
now jonquils
fill the roadside
she remembers
yellow roses/a beginning
in a long narrow box
yellow is for trust
i never send them   zita said
but roses suit you so
what was needed
time enough to answer
breathtaking words
like jazz licks
what she needed
was a sail   staunch
as yellow roses
to keep them from drift

now on the road
she can hear the whisper
of impending loss
zita driving   up ahead
silk scarf at her neck
waving near the wheel
while she follows
one last time
in a dented rental car
just so close
as not to lose her
she follows
as words fly off/
punctuate the highway
with grief at the neck
or is it simply resignation
indigo and shivering

eclipse

what mattered then
in that amour
that other life
re-sparks erratic
in this dimension
and will appear
like floating orbs
in the eye of a camera
or right before   or after
flashes of this new affair
the subtle similarities
the head and tail
of what she's searching

show up simply
unexpected
like ordinary magic
another raven soaring by
a hint of wing
along the vault
as if there were already
just enough light
just enough days left
now and now
disclosing everything

she travels in deep space

city or country
dreams again
ravens and perennial trance
how this century
pitches and falls
like any other
how the next day
mounts and shuts
like any other
transient as water
seeping through
the bonsai on the sill

how easily she rolls
the shade
enticing particles of light
ordinary   real as flesh
how easily her elbow crooks
and catches
how personal reflects externals
synchronicity of hebrew letters
tattooed on her hand
the letters on her hand
read NES
translate to miracle
she riffs
her fingers tracing
green and black ink
under a layer of skin
why does her pulse flare
cheboom cheboom

already there are omens
even in the cuffs of night
which gathers   folds itself
through portholes
saturates like music
she wades through hours

detached measures
of illumination
out of body
she writes in her sleep
the night tips
dreams split/recombine
whorls of time
scatter into nothing
a simple twist
of wing or word
nightmares or
the ordinary miracle
of moments
rapping and repeated
cheboom cheboom
cast as far
as any eye can see
and copied down

florida

what day is this

she ponders out loud
it's 45 mph
on this road
knee deep in the keys
the highway's wavy
slow heat like syrup
what's an hour
or a month
can't really say here
nothing better to do
while they slog through
key largo
than count license plates
passing aimless
as anoles
what day is this
how about wednesday
she muses
at the gulf coast sun
watching it drop
noiseless
on the next set of palms
wilting   in the side view
as she signals for a turn

she's on vacation

with someone new
vaguely familiar
with a french disposition
how did they end up here
vaguely familiar
two scorpios
just enough secrets
doling out tease
daring each other
to ditch the distance
kick up the stakes
and while they spoon
(queen size bed
blond headboard)
in the bungalow
gulf side
topography and time
lie somehow beached
between them
the days stretch over
like membranes
like they made a pact
to jump galaxies
she and the woman of france
and their chancy affair

now there are
too many detours
off the seven mile bridge
too much fast food neon
nights are restless
muddy dreams that don't scan
from which she wakes
and wonders
what place is this
what offbeat fragrance
what necessary compass
did she neglect to pack

insomnia crawls

over long boat key
washing out like sand
after almost a week
she settles in
beach glows citrine
gulls get busy
on the shoreline
by late afternoon
she goes swimming
more than once
with the woman of france
they strip
they cast off scales
and through the waves
they pour like divers
holding hands
no matter what floats briny
or how memory repeats
and what seems new
is merely retro
even this far south

time swings

open   at her feet
could this be yesterday/
ten years ago

she watches
the woman of france
on the bungalow porch
(circa 1950's)
dipping watercolors
clear as fresh fruit
winding fingers
through her coral hair

the woman of france
looks up
and smiles
maybe distant still
it's hard to tell
in this raw sun
details go milky
the smile is remarkable
blinks on and off
hypnotic
somehow reminiscent

the sojourn of another mouth
the lapping of another voice
against the shore

the next day

waves pearl out
before the moon waxes
time is ultramarine
undetermined deep
in unplumbed water
somewhere else
a beam shines (trancelike)
they swim
for the lighthouse   she
and the woman of france
toss their bodies
browned   on the rocks
swim back in sync
before the roofs go black

all night they chart
their own cosmology
all night they woo
like time   or death
is pushing at the wall

love snags

when they stop
to pay attention
global news
from off the keys
in summer '99
is shrill   violent
always somewhere
blind atrocities

as the new century
bobs and dips
like an unformed fetus
she reaches far inside
the woman of france
she curls her hand
firms herself around
the core like a glove
everything holds
a home   a world rebuilt
on kundalini
at least just here   just now
where everything
uncoils and fits

her dreams invert

she slides her arms back
over time
as if she needed
to retrieve something
a scrap of hindsight/foresight
particles of sclera from
raven's third eye

she dreams of
ancient hebrew letters
the ones tattooed
on her hand
in her dream
they levitate
words are fate flecked/
mystical
sounds are consonants
vowels filled in by breath

she dreams
there is a kiss
with the woman of france
that lasts for centuries
or is it any kiss
fed into ether
replayed   replayed
she reaches out
she grabs for it
when it ignites
as comets burn
there's no conclusion
how it started
in what language
or from where

montreal

"Time has passed over me," she thought, trying to collect herself; .... "How strange it is! Nothing is any longer one thing. I take up my handbag and I think of an old bumboat woman frozen in the ice. Someone lights a pink candle and I see a girl in Russian trousers."

Virginia Woolf, *Orlando*

april 2000

insomnia again
she's vigilant
specks of phantoms
in the iris
past love clings like silt
nights pass surreal
forming ink blots
time curves
the energy   external
bloats/blisters
manhattan's crimson/
gory   trachea slashed
or is that next year
according to the hopi
all time is present now
the air is limp
with leaving/
what's left behind
and she can't imagine
anything else

time and distance bend
the woman of france scoops her
over latitudes
for a tryst in montreal
an antique room in *vieux port*
old city   brass bed
an olive swath of window silk
early buds of celadon
across the avenue

auberge du vieux port

has casement windows
trusts that time
floats back   to 1880's
once a warehouse
then a saddle shop
fronting the river
commodious   enduring

from their old city room
suggestion smears the pane
her lover has gone out
or lies next to her
or is also writing
this might be hallucination
herself disjointed
remnants of french verbs
from another year
another life
(who was she with then)
listing on her tongue

in this bilingual city
sounds tangle and wrap
she listens for the trill
the subtle hum
to lift her like a drug
the sky outside
bronze/tarnished
(as if it's hung like this
for decades)
the sky inhales
as she disrobes in english
(who does she want now)
loosing questions
sometime soon her lover asks
or answers
the room   the sky
la chambre   le ciel

landscape moving closer
past/future
place resembles place
she pivots south
where pictures mesh
and slivers of manhattan
quiver in the glass

she lifts her pen

she writes
dear woman of france
time slows here
taking us hostage
difficult to touch you
in *vieux port*
where sepia clings pale
as yesterday's wine
difficult to follow curves
of cobblestone
unsteady
where we place our feet

here   we are the mist/
the maze
ça roule montréal
we spin like separate globes
and in the dark
i reach for you

beyond   the city lies
reversible/permutable
two tongues
two transitory histories
the room is bathed
in tapestry   illusory
and each of us
gropes desperately
for symmetry
as proof that we exist

she writes again

dear zita
you travel in space
like chi
looping windward
you wait for pathway
reentry
like patience itself
you wait for cool rain
or smoky tea
just before evening
something of comfort
perfuming the hour
the tenor of your voice
like brighton by the sea
saliferous and irresistible

in montreal
you shadow fervor
lacing of words/bodies
verge of moments
tactile in transit
absorbed like soil
under the table legs
you're here   there
whatever destination
i encounter
and you wait   patient
as the draw of breath
in the long nape of corridor
above muted april water
wherever things begin
to move   you come
riding the nippy air
circling time

love plays at her

on piano keys
on strings   on drum
bold plunging notes
personify
what was/who is
they mingle and rise
what did she always want
(who does she dare
to want now)
noir intense
with raven wings
love flies at her
from the doorway
the beams
the window sash
bewitching her shoulders
the texture all zita
and the woman of france
all crashing
through her lungs
in heady gust
of a crescendo

montreal midnight

she drops her body
over hers
sifts through lineaments
and skin
for shades of meaning
there is a breast here
there is an opening
there is a hunger
there is an easy journey

after this night
the first thing she'll recount
is how the sky lightens
with a gilded edge
like a paris sky   she muses
but can't be sure
or find a fast enough way
to translate

who is this woman
this woman of france
who stretches from the hip
and catches her midair
and always catches her
midair   and never misses

she drops her body
spreads and lingers
as the night always has
(she's sure of this)
she reads the air
for signs/promises
she promises to read aloud
and does
lips echo lips   hips press
this interlude
this mirrored blaze
this woman   who

this moment
stretches from the hip
and catches her
mid sentence   or midair
the night or moon
with such seductive
hesitation
just begun to climb

later on

the voice between them
builds
like a slow swinging bridge
as they carry precious stories
on their tongues

predawn

drapes velvet
sounds like muffled horn
runs the notes   unbrushed
all over town
before the stir of *vieux port*
she's staring at a memory
shelter island 1992
before the woman of france
she's at fresh pond
chet baker in her ears
the laze of zita
in a lawn chair
mid afternoon
(who did she want then)
zita   with indigo hair

she reads
whomever we annihilate/
adore
reflects the past
she writes that here
there's no duality
the eye of montreal is overlap
the air   the dreams
interchangeable
polyphony inside her head
preconscious
how much love
to counter cataclysm/
feel safe
she's superstitious

the truth of it
she writes
she wants them both
the truth of it
that language manifests a life
she dreams bilingual

it's all about improvisation
how to fuse all this love
how to swim to the port
and the port
and keep from drowning

dementia

day by day

her mother dissolves
slips away
into another world
another country
called dementia
leaving traces
of forgotten speech
like ticket stubs
her mother travels
time and space
like she was made for it
a real pro
month by month
the daughter follows suit
aboard a speeding train
her mother
moon by moon
like hazy scenery
whooshing by

cholom

often now
the mother sleeps
the daughter visits weekends
wakes her   docile as a child
dresses her
then takes her out to eat
this is a *cholom*
a walking dream

oh my god
the mother says
whenever
the daughter drops by
as if she came upon
a lost soul/a cousin
from delancey street or essex
from the old days
in the neighborhood
down on the lower east side

cholom 2

she dreams repeatedly
that her mother lifts off
buoyant/unhurried
not like her father did
the premonition at 13
she couldn't shake
next year he was dead
fast as frost
in the dreams
her mother's going slow
to compensate
treading atmosphere
kite-like
her shell limbs
angling out for altitude
short trips/free fall
licking pinkie to the breeze
for easy navigation

assisted living

senior quarters
in queens
is her mother's new address
sometimes on a visit
they play scrabble
in the lounge
at the cherry card table
(sinatra croons in the background)
and her mother's a rogue
she might do anything
unassisted
her eyes twinkle
then she winks
as if to say
she'll maybe cheat
or steal a few
(the x   the z   the q)
like she still wants
that badly to win

2

october 14 2000

she finds her mother
sitting at the foot
of the bed
(pink taffeta behind her)
hearing aid missing
wearing giant earphones
instead
looking somehow
like a teenage homey
on the uptown express

do i look crazy
asks the mother
as if the daughter

would really know
how to answer

    3

november/december 2000

the weather is bleak
pillars of cold   numbing
what she can't name
there are weeks
and weeks
the daughter doesn't visit
visions of the mother
shrinking
in her tiny room
keep her away
it isn't about
right or wrong anymore
she thinks
it's something insuperable
like the ice giving way
(or a building)
under your feet

after the breach
she doubles
her trips to queens
and then goes shopping
in eccentric stores
exotic coffees/sweets
black licorice for her mother
and a zen fountain
so she can lose herself
to water
beading down the sides
like liquid wood
when she gets home

one day

it feels like night
upended
ashy where
they walk and walk
past the diner
and the paris hotel
they turn the corner
but the mother is lost
where do i live
she asks
and twirls around

her hands shake
(actress hands)
i want to go back
to new york
she cries
i need to be near you
her voice cracks
her eyes fade
like soda fizz
they walk and walk
the wind yowls
a branch snaps
the awnings flap
outside
the daughter's braced
inside   she's faulty pipes
bursting

another day

the mother's flushed
all askew
in the hallway
and on a wing chair
waiting
she wears red paisley
tights below her dress
black pumps
her bra undone
below her breasts
the daughter pops them in
the mother
doesn't miss a beat
a cheshire smile
like this was something
they were used to
every morning

later   they have omelets
in the perky dining room
for lunch
then stroll around the block
of forest hills
like real travelers
old companions
arm in arm
the mother isn't weak
or moaning
so they settle
at the garden fence
where sun is
daughter snapping photos
mother posed
with jade green grass
cars strung out   like diamonds
sparkling down the parkway

birthday

july sixteenth
almost a century of dreams
like too many boats
steering at once
through the mother's head
traffic jams on the water
thinks the daughter
sitting across from her
in the shiny greek diner
a giving in to time
on their faces
a mini mocha cake
and decaf
an icing of miles
a wilderness of candles
between them

something holds

the mother here
she stays past ninety
teaching nuance
and interpretation
she changes cadence/voice
like switching stations
flits to calendars   bygone
or somewhere between pages
so her story stops
and starts in other places
on certain days
she lets the daughter in
for the ride
moving breakneck   flat out
keener than anything
but love
the daughter does her best
to keep up

cusp 2003

it's march and
the mother's been moved
to a rest home
in lake mary
just outside orlando
where she hangs out
with death
until the daughter arrives
the day is bleached
time stalls
now the mother
waves the daughter in
her gloved hands raised
with incantation
her eyes
dancing coal
the leafy fabric
of her chair aglow
the tumor in her belly
swelled like calla lily
the day is bleached
time stalls
the daughter's heart
is pumping wild jargon
the mother's ruby afghan
cloaked about her
the daughter clings
releases/clings
her heart rips
she can't find her voice
the mother's fingers
waving words
her chalky lips
pressing   i love you
mouthing   take me home
her face   all gold

broad as sunflowers
her eyes burning
up the day
through the sun porch

   2

here   in this room
now or just before
time moves   pacific
now or just before
the daughter cradles   close
(enough to read the age spots
on her mother's skin)
remembers
there are 72 names of god
the kabbalists found
72 shapes of sound
from the seat
where breath lives
to the lips
where letters spiral
into space
now or just after
she recites her mother's name
72 times
and listens to her breathe

names

lilyan libba libby lilly lib
mother mom mama ma *mamaloshen*
vos machs du mine mamaleh
a ve bis du
vos danks du

mama ma ma mama *mamaleh* ma ma
a ve gaystau
libbymama mama ma ma ma mommy mama
mama ma *mamanu*
ma ma ma ma ma ma
mamamamamamamamamamamama
mamamamamamamamamamamama
mamamamamamamamama   ma ma

freeze frame

later
swimming laps
in the pool
of the flamingo motel
comes the grey stroke
of night   cinereous
a tone ruffling
undetectable
or a fine stain   surfaced
like breeze
as her arms brush/
break water
break water
repetitive and slick
and her mother passes

memorial

march 16
beth david cemetery
in elmont new york
a salty haze   quiescent
off jamaica bay

there are
silver streaks
on the caduceus
of the gravestone
of her father
marble   incandescence
a private invitation
where she leans

there is mink
and there is umber
in the imprint of loss
as she stoops
at the graveside
of her mother

the seed brown smell
of fresh turned earth
still tarries
moments cease
and reappear

all so couched
so sheltered
that she takes it
as a marker
unconditional/beckoning
to stay and rest
beside them
for a while

long island: east end

country

it could be any year
but it's 2000
time forgets itself
when she's alone here
writing in zita's house
northwest woods
below sag harbor

what did nevelson say
my whole life's been late

the house enfolds her
clockless
soft cedar skin
supporting glass
a week of this
and she transforms
diaphanous

the walls melt
she peers
from any room
veiled mien of morning
ochre afternoon
a week of this
the silence sets
from any room
it sings like pastoral
later   on the phone
she'll mention none of this
or what comes after
how days start fading
and she's seeing things
the stare at trees
who stare back
how march buds tease
and hold like tendons

not much moves
or happens
in the old sense
she's clear/transported
wowed by real time
bare bones of spring
where silence sets itself
and stays

night scene

black swallows day
behind the deck
she flips the switch
displays an acre of woods
enchanted
and someone's outline
smacks of her father
undead
far as a high fly
on the vapory road
her mother's form
is easier to guess
in glitter blond
before dementia

staring hard
she pegs her parents
posed like frozen deer
among the trees
her mother   chic
in mauve chambray
her father
in that wall-to-wall grin
and slouched fedora

why have they come
so present tense/serene
to keep her company
she fancies
intoxicating
the feel of them
as they approach
with time unsprung
so she can trace
how memory transfigures
like a clip of stills
suspended
over what it gleans

m.d.

her father   dad   daddy
boris   benjamin
beryl   ben
left-wing country doctor
risked abortions
delivered babies
on his day off
when she was small
he sang her lullabies
until he fell asleep

when she was older
he took her
on house calls
where she'd haul his black bag
snapped and zippered
bulky   bulged
with needles/ointments
pads with numbers
for prescriptions
charmed compartments

he was like houdini
she   his intern
now she wants
examination/diagnosis
conjured cures
for the millennium

but all she can recover
are his baggy suits   expansive ties
how his biceps bounced
in rhythm
(stethoscope dangling)
how he told yiddish secrets
to her mother
and always smelled
of medicines/sweet
unfiltered pall malls

diva

her mother   born libba
born ostrogursky
on hester street
always fancied violet
and drama
(this is how she sees her)

in english school
they changed her name
to lilian
taught her how to write
right handed   palmer method
her life made circles
so she waited   slightly dizzy
married late
her high school sweetheart

who she followed to vermont
to burlington
colonial new england
callous winters
where she kept kosher
read voracious
starred in temple plays
became queen esther/
purim's hero
freed her people
all across the stage and back
with scarves
and sexy open toes
(this is how she sees her)
with circling gestures
like a diva

and saved up her children
for later

another night

her parents vanish
as spirits do
but there's a masked raccoon
over the damp deck
roof walking
curling into eaves
from the rain
she lowers lamps
and likes to think
(at least) it's warm up there
and likes to match
that wanderlust
that pitchy smolder
up against the pane

she arches   birdlike
sharp eyed and glossy
the will to fly
is in her bones
alignment
long wing span
between lines
the point they intersect
the scope of world below
and hers   defined
the reckless pull
of temporal and beyond

vermont

blizzard

just before or after 1995

the dates descend
she's in vermont
where she is from
but hasn't been
for years

winter now
she passes fields of snow
thick distances of white
(the car wheels skid and bray)
long memories and snow
over everything
tugging down
to the root
quieter than death
which stole her father
lynx quick
snow caps froze
new york yanked her away

(in the telling and retelling
figures change
like snowflakes
like shadow on snow)
at least that's how
she remembers it

snowed in

three days
whiter than metaphor
snow-blind
she draws her darling
to her
up and down this tiny peak
but she can never
really say
how it is to be back

vermont is like you
she suggests
to the woman of france
entrancing
a nitid calling
from another room
a door ajar

eyes shut
she knows this terrain
this contour by touch
your face   she says
touching her now
is full
of earlier and future stars
close so close
i feel myself inside you
yet i can hardly measure
where you are

what she sees

the inuits knew
there are not enough words
in a place like this
to define white
it left them breathless
what did they see
before naming
sugar snow
salt-like
soft packed powder
naked of intention
apun   is snow
here   it's audacious
this white
posed on hips of mountain
pressed like fingertips
at the corners
of a mouth
this white
which falls like petals
which falls   breathless
on its belly
she inhales
the smell of white
elixir
she inhales   pure past
like pure incline
like slope
and what she sees
in all this white
is passage
then pure drop
euphoric still
nothing after

what she can do

she can return
wide-eyed
like a tourist
rove neighborhoods
locate houses
she lived in
on handy court
south prospect street
the synagogue
the hospital
where her father practiced
but she can't connect
her heart
or find the thread
to suture
there's still a wound
raw as lake champlain
at winter solstice

so she returns
like an ellipsis
someone native
with an accent
nearly local
but whose name
now comes up
on a guest list/
three day reservation
signing in
and later   signing out

what they do

this night or that
on bolton mountain
at the black bear inn
they watch
the snow shaped vans
like vistas
a fire stove cooks
the double room
the patchwork quilt
is lit   they leave
and walk until the cliff
the snow does flips/
takes up so much space
they talk of it
the snow amazes
moon perched there
at least til two
they dress alike
except for one red hat
and hike uphill
consumed with white
until the moon lets go
behind the lift
while   glaciers in peru
and argentina
slowly crack and shift

what she prefers

here
is how weather happens
how sheets of it
cut across windshields
shimmer fierce/indefectible
how everything is
penciled in and
up the road a-piece

vermont is bantam
feisty   narrow framed
like she is
anomaly   eccentric
how its mountains
adhere   go green
without formality

this is a self-styled life
says the cross-country man
rangy as pines
reading her mind
over his shoulder
pushing his poles
pointing skis   resplendent
at the wind

what she crosses

is time
in the daydream
lined with slender maples
as her father's ghost
crunches snow/
turns the wheel
of his desoto

over thirty years
and she breathes herself
into the passenger seat
buries her head
in his wide lapels
she falls   (not asleep)
into overdrive
time overtakes her
(how many fathers
she wonders
downed   in lhasa/kabul)

now he's roused   he's back
her own daddy
dashing doctor
touch of raymond massey
maybe benny goodman
round the eyes
his smile   hers
his barrel chest   as close
as she will ever come
reclaiming all of it

what she finds

up front
on pearl street
loose bricks
on what used to be
her father's office
and time is full
of black holes
january
the month he died
there is absence
in the present
(loose blues
like leftover change)
down the hill
battery park
is crowned with ice
the air   streaked copper
harsh beauty
all the same
as it was then
particulars surrendered
and dispersed
at the horizon

what she leaves

burlington
is contradiction
birthplace
that buried her father
she walks it
like you talk
a first language
you haven't spoken
since childhood
she tastes nostalgia
bitter/tinny
as coffee standing
too long
in a burned pot
on a weekend's borrowed stove

a storm   a dazzler
blows through
hides the entrance
of a trendy mall
she never knew
this is what it means
to scale illusions
in your mind
she tells herself
then descend
to real exits
you traverse
as cool and unscathed
as you can

and what she takes

she leaves vermont
tracking snow
thin layer of recall
under her feet
like magic carpet
inside   her lungs puff
the white enters
and stays
she gives it pause
she gives it room   and more
to spread

new york

The only reason for time is so that everything doesn't happen at once.
Albert Einstein

prelude

september 1   2001

eight days sojourn
the woman of france
shows her paris/
premiere
the city is resonance
reflected sound
in this *arrondissement* or that
the supple moan of history
primal as sex
how light fixes itself
to buildings across water/
how easily she could stay
and recreate time
as they all did
(streams of artists)
lift layers of past
like paint
draw weathered frontage
through her hand
she floats *le bateau mouche*
under twelve bridges
like separate worlds
animate
under one night's slated sky
here   she could discover
how to handle anything
with ambiance/
panache
even an avalanche of horror
ten days later   in new york

september 11 2001

that morning cropped
the tropospheric shriek
and tilt
new york electro shocked
in razor daylight
what time was it
what déjà vu
was this
prefaced by the mayans
the hopi
how to deconstruct carnage
without remove
can she say
she was removed
with zita on long island
that early tuesday
can she retrace
the streak of blue jay
from the woods
before they watched tv
their dumbstruck eyes
as wingless bodies flew
and fragments fell
to rubble
she'd surfed for weather
could she deny
the sudden freeze
her toes and fingers numb
the click   her private
instant memory of loss
could she have guessed
what happened next
the sheer surreal
might ever have been
making love   or breakfast

september 12

manhattan

she exits the bus
west 99th street
and doesn't recognize
the smell   her city
the smoke and ash
frosted over concrete
like childhood snow
on vermont mountains
but this is flat white
so flat it doesn't breathe
she begins to sense things
not easily there
the scrunched foreground
wrenched background
dull stares where sight was
gotham gutted in grief
the crush the silence
the pall the stun
the shrouded stop sign
the wicked chill
the dense fog   opaque
over all of it
the absolute hush
cradling broadway
like an iron lung

october 1

lucidity gone
is it dawn or dusk
the days reel
out of whack
skittish/edgy
and everyone's tired
of watching what's invisible
she sleeps
as much as she can
pressed to the woman of france
new york's embraced
by white dust and flags
like warnings
hardly anyone dares
past their neighborhood
the city shrinks
to tomb size
and all bets are off

november/april 2002

new york is bloodless
as an old film
countless frames of grey

for months
time erases itself
energy drains and clogs
in half empty bottles
on stale birthday cakes
settles into closets/
stairwells
on greenwich and chambers
under the triborough
through the hudson tunnel
seeping into 5th and 6th
and 7th avenues

it nudges brownstones
filling subway and bus
blurring   with cement
like congested crust
the city enters spring
on its knees
behind pulled blinds
and filtered lenses
darker than before
but morning is still
morning   after all
rising open mouthed
and eager
for a hint of grace

vertigo

in a flashback
she's high
higher than sequoias
ephemeral
that raven thing again
she passes glaciers
global scan
or divination
willing them to cleave
in the faltering 'scape
she ducks   free fall
a spread of clouds
like cards
all read september 9th/
10th   in spades
hoist before the plunge
toes taut   pre dive
(pre birth pre bomb)
lynching   holocaust
fever on the run
earth about to waffle
at the brink
cosmic rift
kaleidoscopic
last give of springboard
blink   before the rifle pull
pinch of a grenade

the telepathic ripple
the uneasy step
before judgment
the startling instant
of choice

earlier

no one's there
in north haven
at the town beach
she bikes to
stony and swayed
like a boomerang
sound whistles through
reverberates
no one's there
the may sun arrowed
in afternoon sky
and no one's even waiting
not a rock out of place
or a boat coasting west
she can claim
as unfamiliar
a burly jeep u turns/
backs off
and some new trap
winds skinny legged
into the bay
that's all
everything else is
just as it was
like nothing happened
last september
when she sat with a radio
pinned to her ear
sorrow still warm/biting
the city all locked up
a broken bastion
floating miles away

later

she'd rather stay
for starlight
past dinner
and watch it fill
the pebbled beach
with hope or fantasy
like movie sets
there's nothing
she'd prefer
than make a month
out of this
maybe a year
memorize the names
of planets
track novas/clusters
from another plane
another century
like it might all
happen differently

dementia 2001

well before september
before florida
her mother's mind crumbles
like a building
(the commonality of space)
now what's left
the chips   emerge
like buoys scraping water

like people after auschwitz
she renders witness
in a city of fog
the bits of paper
surfacing like dried blood
or code
refracted angles
where collective/
unconscious collide

her mother's tumbling words
extended prayers
(the breath starts here)
the scent of lilies
on the ground
(her mother's scent)
pronounced intangible

downtown
2000 spirits waver
at the pit
her mother's voice
(the commonality of sound)
now marked and audible
now   altogether missing

coda new york

time compresses/expands
downtown
the wound remains
like monument
a vast gulp of dirt
wasted and pale
uptown
on the bike path
near the highway
in the west 50's
trump towers
fill in like smog
an emptiness
where heart was
revamped/revived
she passes skeletons
of steel jetty
straddling the river
ribs and twisted digits
pulling far offshore
beyond the bend
a rush of dandelions
polished benches
bobbing houseboats
small things remind
like scars
the odor here
is sorrow charred/
washing through the veins

navaho 2002

in july (her mother's month)
she's gone again
needing west
all the way to arizona
where the earth's flesh
lays dreamlike
why does her throat catch
is it the angle of allure
the naked sweep
of side by side peaks
undraped torsos
of tree line/rocks
roll and heave
of creamy bottomed mesas
over canyons
like welcoming thighs

further on
sonoran desert
and the sky runs wild
goes wide screen
like a drive-in movie
the rocks go red
this is navaho land
the mountain is a mountain
she and the woman of france
like virgin country
the soles of their feet
firm as the ground
the tops of their scalps
weightless

and further still
arroyos split bajadas
echoes of clouds
glance off stone
and slow air
birds swim through

maybe ravens
the gaze is soft
the tint is revelation
the mountains stand fast
the heat rises

anima

back east
manhattan somnambulate
months pile up
like towers
shards of time cut
blotches in the skyline
are we found
or uncomfortably lost

time shuffles
the souls lift
it is again september
at the boat basin
where she sits cross-legged
like a yogi docked
as dusk unfurls
and the street lamps
flicker a jig

this night
she invokes ravens
mimics their acuity
their longing
poised on tiptoe
flaps her wings
floats like apparition
over longitudes
in and out of port

she will become a map
barometer
capture subtle change
of centuries and climes

breath gathered at her throat
inhale   exhale
wings slant
curb the corners

of what could be
north or south
aerial/balanced
she's iridescent
below she visions water
stretching   swooping back
she pitches low
into a glide

the message waits the courier
as stars whirl thudless
through the void

taos

Slowly wheeling, like the rays of a searchlight, the days, the weeks, the years passed one after another across the sky.
Virginia Woolf, *The Years*

1

august   new mexico
2004 or 5 or 6 or

somewhere   there is war
in cities with melodious names
nairobi   gaza   karachi   baghdad
eyes gouged and bleeding
bodies akimbo
somewhere   gaseous fumes
devour land mass
temperatures pike off the map
somewhere   in new orleans
veins of water break
blues play themselves out
but not here   not now

2

taos is a time warp
enchanted desert town
a fringe of the world
what is she doing at this altitude
reality altered
the mix of red clay   sweet grass
the blazing wild palette
latticed clouds   like o'keefe's
taos is the mountain
porous and holy
omniscient in navaho

3

it's said that
taos mountain welcomes you
or spits you out
on saturday
the mountain sings to her

on saturday
she travels to the pueblo
leaving time at the gate
centuries of moments
1000 years
of red willow people
unbroken
acres and acres
and the sacred blue lake
stolen/returned
by u.s. government
1000 years of tiwa
spoken   never lost
or written down

   4

she dreams   east
her college students
animation majors
bombarded with media/
images   desensitized
sketching themselves
into oblivion
drawing cartoons
on their jeans   t-shirts
every figure magic markered
every bubble
hanging lonely
waiting to be filled
in her dream
the clock bleeds
she studies taos mountain
for a remedy
something mixed
with lavender/tenderness
to leap out and save them

5

on sunday   or monday
a sleeve of purple sage
at the doorway
rubs adobe
notions of legacy
and visitation
her mother again
her friend rhonda
(who taught her new mexico
who taught nothing's linear
then died on a winding road
of southern colorado)
they're here
beyond mythology
soothing her from nightmares
her mother offering a nosh
rhonda beaming
in her san cristobal garden
at how things unfold

6

this night   she dreams
they're all here
or is it tomorrow
or next year   or the next
she and zita
and the woman of france
each of them   wanderers
descended from nomads
at the base of their spines
each of them   rootless

what are they doing
the three of them
in this reverberant casita

lining the narrative
with flavors of sustenance
slicing of warm bread
and radishes
roasted chili peppers
hint of spice/fresh dill
vintage pinot noir
on the table
breathing in and out
keeping faith
in slow easy rituals

   7

afternoon   siesta
a town softens into itself
lightening surfs the courtyard
urging the moments
to change
the edges to let go
and glitter
like a grove of aspens

she dreams
or is it almost sunset
as they race the rio grande
white water whips
downstream
they shoot the box
they aim/
lean into the mountain
watching it go
impossible pink
then brass and sterling
in the walking rain

8

time gyrates possibility
the vociferous light show
one star   one moon can make
behind a ridge
if the eye spans wide
and the energy is right

how much love
can they surrender
without fear or memory
to impair them
the places where it lacked
attended to
exposed like solar etchings

what does it mean
to be more than blood
more than consciousness
what does it mean
to practice wonder
prepare another meal
in a world posed to go under

she peers closer
at the women she adores
their chests billowing
like ravens   capricious
they can fly
release anything
this is the time
in between
what went before the promise
this century made
and the piercing
unknowable truth
of what comes after

9

see three lovers
a multitude
a celebration
endangered
see the poem
the prairie dog
the appaloosa
the ridge nosed rattler
the bald eagle
the whooping crane
the gray wolf
the silvery minnow
the grasshopper sparrow
the jumping mouse
the pecos sun flower
the double rainbow
the swirling nebula
she exclaims
as if they will all
soon   be extinct
as if they are
miracles   just born
and time wheels
around them

www.ingramcontent.com/pod-product-compliance
Lightning Source LLC
Chambersburg PA
CBHW030331080526
44584CB00012B/819